IMAGES
of England

BOOKHAM AND FETCHAM

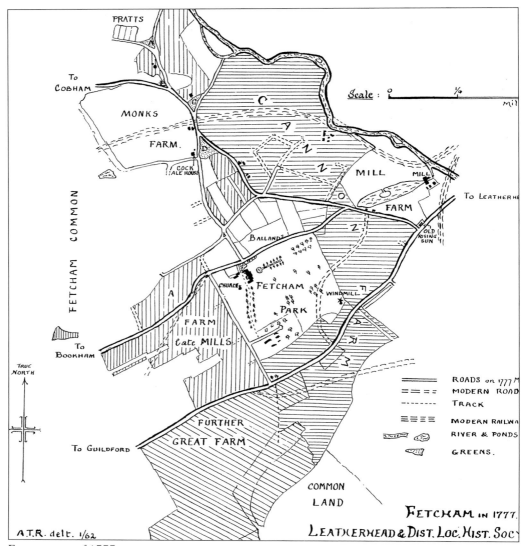

From a map of 1777.

IMAGES
of England

BOOKHAM AND FETCHAM

Compiled by
Linda Heath
on behalf of
the Leatherhead and District Local History Society

TEMPUS

Acknowledgements

I should like to express my thanks to the many people who have helped with the compilation of this book in various ways. In particular, I should like to thank Brian Godfrey, Alan Pooley and Ed Tims for the information for the captions; Stephen Fortescue and Goff Powell for the generous use of their photographs; and Gwen Hoad for making copies of the photographs of the Wales family.

My thanks are also due to all those who helped by supplying information and by lending or copying photographs – especially to the following: Mrs M. Adams, Mr D. Banham, Mrs E. Crellin, Mr E.W. Culley, Miss A. Doughty, Mrs S. Eaton, Mrs C. Fairclough, Father Jelft, Mr H.G. Knowles, Mr E. Leat, Mrs G. Morley and Ms M. Lewington of the *Leatherhead Advertiser*, Mr A. Mason, Mrs G. McKenzie, Mrs J. Morgan, Mrs H. Mummery, Mr S. Poulter, Surrey Industrial History Group, Mr P.A. Tarplee, Mr M. Wanstall, Mrs G. Williams.

Cover photograph: A group outside the old Rising Sun, Fetcham, 1922.

First published 1999, reprinted 2005

Tempus Publishing Limited
The Mill, Brimscombe Port,
Stroud, Gloucestershire, GL5 2QG
www.tempus-publishing.com

British Library Cataloguing in Publication Data.
A catalogue record for this book is available from the British Library.

ISBN 0 7524 1825 4

Typesetting and origination by Tempus Publishing Limited.
Printed in Great Britain.

Contents

From a map of 1897.

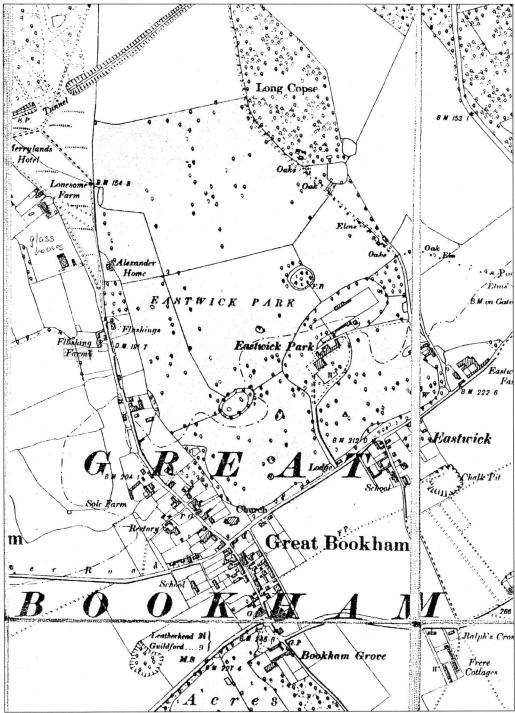

From a map of 1897.

Introduction

Members of the Team

This book has been a team production by several members of the Leatherhead & District Local History Society and my thanks to them and to others are recorded in the Acknowledgements. However, some of our members have played such a key role that their names must be mentioned here. Brian Godfrey produced virtually all the information about Bookham, and Ed Tims and Alan Pooley did the same for Fetcham and I am extremely grateful to them. Most of the photographs in this book belong to the Local History Society, but Stephen Fortescue and 'Goff' Powell have both been extremely generous in allowing me unlimited use of photographs and postcards from their private collections. To them also I cannot express my thanks enough.

About the Photographs

It is perhaps stating the obvious to say that any book of photographs depends upon the pictures available. What strikes one when going through any collection is the wealth of pictures of certain places or buildings and the total dearth of others. This, of course, depends on two things – the actual collection of photographs and also whether the subjects were ever photographed at all. So the collection in this book is necessarily compiled from the photographs available. Some of these have already appeared in other publications such as S.E.D. Fortescue's *People and Places* and *The Story of Two Villages* and in the recent *History of Fetcham* published by our Society in 1998. But I have tried to find as many photographs as possible which have not appeared in other books.

Readers may well wonder why their favourite place or building is not included in this book, and almost certainly the reason will be that I did not have an old photograph of it. Sometimes one is unable to use an extremely interesting photograph of people because there is nothing to tell one who the people were, when it was taken or what the occasion was. This is always very tantalizing. Sometimes I had to hazard a guess about certain things, and if it turns out that this was not correct, I shall be only too pleased to have the mistake rectified.

About the Book

In this book I have treated Great Bookham, Little Bookham and Fetcham as three separate villages. In a perfect world, one would like to have an equal number of photographs for each village within each chapter, but this was not always possible. However, the photographs for each village are as evenly balanced as I could make them. The photographs cover the centres of each village rather than the outlying areas on the parish boundaries, such as Polesden and Slyfield.

In arranging the photographs within each chapter, I have tried to take the reader for an imaginary walk through each village and on to the next, so that there is a geographical progression from one village to another. It was not always possible to do this absolutely accurately, but this was the general idea.

Finally, I can only hope that the reader will obtain as much pleasure, interest and amusement in going through these glimpses of a bygone age as I have had in compiling them.

Linda Heath, 1999.

One
General Views

Leatherhead Road, Great Bookham, 1905. Ralph's Cross, the three-storey high cottages on the corner of Crabtree Lane, were named after Ralph Sutherland, who is said to have been hanged here in the early eighteenth century for sheep rustling from Polesden Lacey. The nearer cottages, partly hidden by the trees, have now been replaced by more modern houses and the children on the right were outside the grounds of Bookham Cottage, also no longer there.

Hawks Hill, Fetcham, 1896. From time immemorial there has been a trackway along this route leading from the River Mole up the hill from Leatherhead to Fetcham and Bookham.

Sandy Lane, Fetcham, 1928. This is now The Ridgeway viewed from the Guildford Road and presents a very rural scene. Park Close and Farm Close are already marked by fingerposts on the left, although no houses have yet been built. These were the first signs of development after the sale of the Fetcham Park estate in 1924. The corn stack is on land which was formerly part of Further Great Farm (see map on p. 2) and the entrance on the right, through the quickset hedge, originally led to a sawmill and a windmill.

Guildford Road, Great Bookham, 1905. This is looking west from a point near the modern footbridge. The nearer house on the right is Hawkwood House which was the home of Alfred Westendarp. Mrs Swann lived at Ballinvey which was a larger house just west of Hawkwood House.

Guildford Road, Great Bookham, in the 1930s. This is looking eastwards from a point just to the west of the present Hawkwood Rise. When the land on the left was sold for housing development, Hawkwood House (on the left behind the hedge) was retained and converted into several flats.

Church Road, Great Bookham, c. 1910. This is looking towards the village from the second bend in the road from the station. In the distance on the right is the Edenside Nursery which was established in around 1891 by James Douglas who became a world authority on auriculas and carnations. The large house, closer to the road, was Elmcroft, built by Andrew West, a local builder at Bennets Farm who employed some fifty men and built many of the houses in Church Road.

Gt. Bookham Common.

Church Road, 1905. This is looking in the opposite direction from a point where the first footpath leaves the road to cross the common towards the station. Few houses had been built on the right of the road at this time. The large house seen through the trees was the home of Richard Lee, the architect responsible for the conversion of the Barn Hall in 1906.

Rectory Lane, Little Bookham, *c.* 1910. Preston House, now the Preston Cross Hotel, is on the right. Although part of the estate of the Manor of Little Bookham, it was tenanted for long periods. For about twenty years towards the end of the nineteenth century it was a boys' boarding school described as 'an establishment for preparing gentlemen for the Army'! Even more surprisingly, it was run by a clergyman, the Revd Thomas Nixon.

CROSS ROADS, LITTLE BOOKHAM.

Preston Cross, Little Bookham, 1908. Not a place to stand and have a chat nowadays! Looking down Little Bookham Street, Half Moon Cottage is visible on the right corner of the crossroads – a sixteenth-century half-timbered cottage which at one time had been used as an alehouse. On the left, Dawes Cottage is just discernible. There were buildings on that side of the street as far down as the Windsor Castle public house.

14

Little Bookham Street, 1905. The first cottage on the left is Dawes Cottage, a sixteenth-century half-timbered dwelling which has recently been renovated. Just visible beyond is the end of a seventeenth-century weather-boarded barn which has since been removed. The sign outside the Windsor Castle can be seen in the distance, quite low down by the road.

Little Bookham Street, 1912. This is looking the opposite way, towards Preston Cross. Rose Cottage, built in the early eighteenth century, is on the right, and two more cottages, now known as Orchard Cottage and Book End, are next in line up the street. At this time these cottages faced open fields on the opposite side of the street.

Church Road, Great Bookham, 1917. This is from a point just south of Sole Farm Road. On the left is the mill with its chimney just visible behind. Before this time it was a steam-operated flour mill, but by the beginning of the twentieth century the premises were used as a timber yard and sawmill. The miller's house is behind the trees on the left.

Lower Road, Great Bookham, 1912. This is looking from the junction of Lower Road with St Nicolas Avenue. The fence and trees on the left formed the boundary of Eastwick Park and the house on the right (now no. 159) had a front door onto the road. On the back of this card a teacher from London wrote 'We took our Juniors to Bookham yesterday, about 210 of us. Oh it was lovely in the country.'

Eastwick Road, Great Bookham, *c.* 1908. The Anchor Inn stands behind the tree on the left and the shed for the cart is just visible on the right. This formerly belonged to Woodcote Farm but is now part of Coach House Cottage. This aspect of the road has not changed much over ninety years and even the brick walls have survived present-day traffic.

Eastwick Drive, Great Bookham, *c.* 1930. This is from a point opposite the house just north of the ponds. These houses, nos 49-61, on the left, were built on farmland which was part of the Eastwick Park estate, sold for building development in the 1920s. Number 61 was the home for many years of Mrs Elizabeth Harrison, who helped to establish the Bookham Community Association.

Kennel Lane, Fetcham, 1918. This view is unrecognizable today. Near the southern end of the lane, Royden Farm was used from about 1800 until 1886 as kennels by the Surrey Union Hunt. Originally its access was from Bell Lane, while Kennel Lane provided a route up to the Cobham Road, now Fetcham Common Lane. A message on the back of this postcard says 'What do you think of this for a honeymoon?'

Lower Road, Fetcham, 1903. The house on the left is the Salt Box at the head of The Street where it joins the Lower Road; the entrance to Fetcham Park House is on the right. The man standing by the hedge is believed to be either the photographer or a local character who owned a tricycle.

The Street, Fetcham, 1906. On the death in 1904 of the Revd Edward Graham Moon, who had been rector for many years, the decision was made to build a new Rectory in The Street. This picture shows it in 1906 just after completion, looking across from what is now School Lane.

School Lane, Fetcham, *c*. 1934. Formerly known as New Road, this road still retains a fine avenue of trees – many of them dating from the time when the land was part of the Ballands Hall estate in the late nineteenth century. When the estate was sold in 1919 the catalogue listed 23 acres of land which was divided into plots. In 1929 this formed the first housing development in Fetcham.

Monk's Green, Fetcham, 1905. The original almshouses are on the right at the junction of River Lane – a farm track leading to the Splash. The Reading Room on the left was built by Squire Hankey in the 1880s as a sort of 'Working Men's Club' where villagers could meet and listen to readings from books and current literature. At the far end of the building is the entrance to the living quarters for the caretaker, which were primitive by modern standards, with an earth floor, a tiny bedroom upstairs and outdoor sanitation. The same view is seen below after 1919 when the War Memorial was erected after the First World War. The memorial was moved in the 1950s to St Mary's church Garden of Remembrance.

Two

Water

Fetcham Mill House and Pond, 1910. There has probably been a mill here since before the Norman invasion and there are several references to a mill on this site from 1293 onwards. This mill was probably constructed in the late eighteenth century and was the most important one in the area. The smaller building in front of the mill house is recorded as being a brew house at some time in the past.

Fetcham Splash in 1895. This shows Randalls Park Estate from the southern branch of the river below the retaining wall or dam. The trees in the background are in the arboretum of Randalls Park House and include a wide variety of native and foreign species planted by former owners who, following the fashion of Victorian times, brought specimens back from their 'World Tour'. Many of these trees have now reached maturity and form a fascinating colour collage in autumn.

Fetcham Splash, 1903. Oldmill Bridge over the River Mole at Fetcham was originally the access from Randalls Road to the mill which, as records indicate, was on the east end of the present island. This mill is mentioned in *Domesday Book*, but no trace of it remains apart from the name. The photograph suggests that the sluice gates on the east side of the bridge directed water through the narrower arch.

Another view of The Splash in 1903. The road from Randalls Road to the mill on the island was extended across the second channel of the river, but as a 'splash' – fordable when the river was low enough or when the sluice gates were open. The wooden footbridge, probably built in the late nineteenth century, provided pedestrian access and survived until replaced by a concrete single span bridge in 1964 and the filling of the approaches to the ford. 'Splashes' were a feature of many shallow rivers and served to strengthen the spokes and rims of horse-drawn vehicles which expanded when wet and so fitted more tightly.

The Mole at Fetcham, *c*. 1905. Sometime during the later half of the eighteenth century Earl Tyrconnel, who owned Randalls Park Estate, decided to put a stop to nearby farm traffic crossing a ford from Cannon Court to the track north of the Common Meadow. He ordered a brick wall to be built at the east end of the island and installed sluice gates below the bridge. He then added a brick dam across the southern arm of the river and obtained the desired effect of the water backing up and rendering the crossing unusable. Farm workers and traffic then had to use the path from Cannon Court through Mole Road and River Lane. One benefit was that the river between Fetcham and Leatherhead could then be used for pleasure boating.

Opposite: Fetcham Mill Pond, 1928. This picture was taken in the years when the Mizen brothers worked their watercress business, using the copious quantities of spring water to grow crops even in winter, as the water emerged at a higher temperature than the river. On the left, the railway bridge and a building alongside for the recently electrified lines through Leatherhead can be seen, and the other railway bridge is seen between the mill house and the cottage.

24

Fetcham Mill Pond, 1909. Both the pond and the island in this picture are larger than they are now, as the water rose from the springs directly underneath. In 1958 the springs were capped, reducing the pond, which is now some distance from its former boundary with the Cobham Road. Beside the mill and the miller's house there is a small boathouse, which suggests that the pleasure boating mentioned under the photograph opposite did indeed take place.

Fetcham Mill Fire, 1917. On 22 August 1917 Fetcham Mill caught fire and was virtually destroyed. The report in the *Dorking Advertiser* of 25 August begins: 'In the early hours of Wednesday morning, a disastrous fire broke out at the well-known mills of Messrs H. Moore & Son of Fetcham, and in a very short time the entire mill was burnt out and considerable damage thereby caused.' The report continued by saying that the fire had been noticed by PC Lewis just after midnight. Leatherhead and Kingston fire brigades were called and after some difficulty, two maids and the gardener were rescued from the mill house, but before he could get upstairs, PC Lewis cut his hand badly on a window and then had to beat off a 'vicious Airedale'. Many helpers had appeared by then and they were able to rescue pigs and cows in nearby sheds, but a horse died in the stable. About 4,000 sacks of grain were destroyed and the total damage was estimated at £4,000.

FIRE AT FETCHAM MILL, AUG. 22, 1917. A. WARREN. PHOTO.

Fetcham Mill Fire. A Leatherhead photographer, Albert Warren, rushed over there to capture the event on film, as can be seen from these photographs.

FIRE AT FETCHAM MILL, AUG. 22, 1917. A. WARREN. PHOTO.

Remains of the mill wheel, c. 1960. After the fire, the mill was abandoned as a working unit and the machinery decayed. Later, the major parts of it, like this wheel, were rescued and put on display. The main driving cogs in this picture are reinforced with metal, but in earlier times they would have been made entirely of wood – probably English elm because of its strength and durability. The remainder of the wheel is cast iron.

A Fowler ploughing engine. This ploughing engine was built in 1886 and had been used to dredge the mud and sediment from Fetcham Mill Pond. In the picture can be seen the winch that drew the cable across a field to which the plough blades were attached. A similar mechanism was adapted for dredging.

Bookham Common, Fish Pond

The Fish Pond, Great Bookham Common. Unlike Fetcham, Bookham has no river Mole flowing through it, but there are several ponds on the common. The Fish Pond is the upper eastern pond of the chain of five ponds across the middle of the common. The common land in Great Bookham had been enclosed in William Keswick's estate of Eastwick Park. After his death, the estate was bought in 1918 by a retired sugar planter who wanted to make money by felling the trees on the land and selling the timber. This resulted in a public outcry, and although the land was sold to a property developer, local residents then managed to purchase Great Bookham Common and present it to the National Trust in 1923.

A Common Pond, Great Bookham, 1927. Bookham Common is now formed from Great and Little Bookham and Banks Commons which together cover 447 acres. Most of the common lies north of Bookham station. There are several ponds which are very similar – the one seen here is probably the lower eastern pond which is next to the Fish Pond in the previous photograph.

Bayfield Pond, Little Bookham Common. This pond lies just north of Bookham Grange Hotel which was originally a private house called Bayfield. The Lord of Little Bookham Manor gave Little Bookham Common to the National Trust in 1924, and the Lord of Effingham Manor gave Banks Common the following year.

Three
Mansions and Some Houses of Note

The Manor House, Little Bookham. This sketch was drawn in the early nineteenth century. The house was built about 100 years earlier and became a school just over 100 years later. For the whole of that period of about 200 years, the Lordship of the Manor belonged to the Pollen family, but they seldom occupied the house and it was let to tenants for long periods.

The Old Rectory, Little Bookham, 1910. The house was built in the eighteenth century and was the rector's home until the turn of the next century. Even in the twentieth century a servant's life could be hard, but one wrote from here in 1910: 'I am getting on alright here. I like Lucy the Cook very much. Bessie the housemaid is going to learn me to ride a bicycle.'

Bayfield, Little Bookham. This house is now the Bookham Grange Hotel on the left of the road which goes over the railway at the north end of Little Bookham Street, just west of Bookham station. It was built in about 1888 on part of Burrough's Farm, owned by Robert Turner, who lived there until around 1900. It then became a nursing home and was occupied by a banking company during the Second World War. It has been a hotel for more than fifty years.

The Grange, Great Bookham. This view is from the south west across the lawn in the early twentieth century. When Arthur Bird, a London solicitor, purchased the house and grounds in 1892, the sale particulars described the estate as 'a very choice freehold property, comprising an attractive residence in the Elizabethan cottage style, approached by a carriage drive.'

The Grange from the north east. This shows the front of the house at the same period with the photograph as a Christmas card. The house became the School of Stitchery and Lace in 1938.

A tea party at The Grange, c. 1895. Mr Bird is on the left with beard and boater, and Mrs Bird is probably the lady pouring tea. She was the daughter of Samuel Shepeard, owner of the famous hotel in Cairo. Their son, George Shepeard Bird, became rector of Great Bookham in 1905. Can he possibly be the boy lolling on the lawn? Or the young man in the boater? The lad in the chair with the dog is obviously too young. Presumably, the two young ladies without hats were the daughters. At this time Rectory Lane ran quite close to the house and Arthur Bird had the lane moved eastwards in 1905.

Arthur Bird JP, *c.* 1907. By this time Arthur Bird had become one of the largest landowners in Great and Little Bookham. He is now chiefly remembered for his gift to the parish of the Old Barn Hall which was on his Sole Farm estate.

The Rectory, Gt. Bookham.

The Rectory, Great Bookham, *c.* 1915. The rector at this time was Arthur Bird's son, G.S. Bird. The house was built in the early nineteenth century on the west side of Church Road, behind where the parade of shops now stands. The house was demolished in 1961.

Above: Fife Lodge, Great Bookham, *c.* 1900. This house, on the east side of Church Road, belonged to Mrs Mary Chrystie, who was a great benefactress to Bookham. She was also a zealous temperance campaigner who bought all the available licensed premises in the area so that alcohol could no longer be sold there. She lived at Fife Lodge from about 1895 until her death in 1911. The house was demolished in 1964.

Bookham Grove, Great Bookham, 1822. There do not appear to be any old photographs of Bookham Grove, but this is from a watercolour by John Hassell and shows the house before the wings were added on. It was built around 1760 and in 1775 it was bought by John Dawney, Viscount Downe, whose family lived there until 1897. It is described in these words by James Edwards in his *Companion from London to Brightelmstone* published at the end of the eighteenth century, soon after John Dawney's death: 'On the south is Bookham Grove, the seat of Viscountess Downe. The house is a handsome brick building which appears of a modern erection and executed in taste; adorned with suitable plantations, good gardens &c, the greatest part of which is surrounded with spacious common fields.'

Below opposite: Mrs Chrystie, *c.* 1900. Mrs Chrystie in her garden at Fife Lodge. As well as her temperance work, she was much concerned about other aspects of village life. She started a penny bank in 1881 to help children to be thrifty and, as a school manager, she encouraged children to develop their talents. She opened a soup kitchen in the village one very hard winter when all the crops had been ruined, and her many gifts included the Victoria Hall in East Street and the recreation ground in the Dorking Road.

Eastwick Park, Great Bookham, 1841. This drawing of the house shows a building that was probably erected by the Howards of Effingham in the late eighteenth century: it was built of brick with a stone dressing. The estate was bought by David Barclay, a son of the owner of Barclay Perkins Brewery, in 1833 and it remained in his family until it was acquired by William Keswick in 1882.

William Keswick MP, 1910. William Keswick held the parliamentary seat for Epsom for thirteen years from 1899. He purchased the Eastwick Park estate in 1882 and lived there until his death thirty years later.

Eastwick Park, Gt. Bookham.

Eastwick Park, 1904. The girl on the lawn in front of the tree is Ivy Keswick when she was four years old. The house faced westward and was approached by a drive from the Lower Road: the new gates to no. 182a Lower Road mark the place where the drive entered the estate. The lodge which stood on the right of the drive was demolished by a bomb in 1940.

Fetcham Park, 1823. This painting by Hassell shows the house as it was originally designed by William Talman. In an article about the house written in 1957, the late Mr F.B. Benger described the nineteenth-century alterations to the building as 'a disaster which has not only robbed us of a work by a leading English architect, but has introduced an alien note into what remains a charming scene.' Not everyone would agree with this opinion, but the original house is certainly a beautifully proportioned building.

Fetcham Park House, 1907. The photograph above shows the front of the building and the one below is the rear view. At this time it was the residence of the squire, John Barnard Hankey, whose family had owned it from the late eighteenth century. It was his family who had the house rebuilt in the 1880s in the style of a small French chateau. In spite of Mr Benger's view of the alterations, it was a fashionable thing to do at that time and the house still retained good proportions and what many people would still consider to be a pleasing exterior. After Hankey's death in 1924 the mansion and twenty acres were sold to become a boys' boarding school.

Ballands Hall, Fetcham, from the east, *c.* 1900. Formerly the Rectory and home of the Moon family, it was built in the late seventeenth century. The majority of the building survives in its original form, but the conservatory and ballroom, dating from the early nineteenth century, were demolished in the 1920s. The house remains one of the impressive treasures of the conservation area.

The Salt Box, Fetcham, *c.* 1920. The Salt Box stands at the corner of The Street and Lower Road and was built in the early eighteenth century. This photograph was taken before an extension was added in 1924. When viewed from The Street, the roof (minus the extension) appears to have a vertical back, horizontal top and sloping front. This shape is reminiscent of the tall boxes with sloping lids which were used to hold salt – hence the name of the house.

The Well House, Fetcham, *c.* 1940. This seventeenth-century house stands on the west side of The Street in an old walled garden. At one time it was part of the offices and estate of Fetcham Park and it is mentioned in insurance papers of 1800. The well, which has long been filled in, lies on the spring line running between Bookham and Fetcham.

Fetcham Cottage, Bell Lane. Quite substantial houses were often described as 'cottages'. This house belonged to the Hankeys of Fetcham Park and was rented by Dr Thomas Monro from about 1795 to 1804. Dr Monro was a physician to George III and was also a great patron of the arts. Many artists visited him here, including Turner, Varley, and Cotman, all of whom painted local scenes while they were there.

Hawks Hill House, Fetcham, *c*. 1905. On the south side of Hawks Hill stands this imposing mansion, one of the few large houses erected in the district in late Victorian years, and home of Sir Edward Blake KCMG, who lived there until 1920. The estate comprised the mansion, two cottages, a lodge and stabling, plus twenty acres of land. When the foundations of the house were dug in 1890, skeletons of twelve very tall Saxon men were uncovered.

Bookham Cottage, Great Bookham, *c*. 1940. This was another substantial house which was called a 'cottage'. Built in about 1898 on the Leatherhead Road, the house is seen here from the west across the lawn adjacent to Mrs Chrystie's recreation ground in the Dorking Road. It was owned by Mr Herbert Allen and after his death in 1944 the house and grounds were auctioned and bought for development to form Allen Road, running north-south across the site.

Four
Cottages and Farms

Timber yard in Little Bookham Street, *c.* 1920. These carts belonged to a timber yard which was at the northern end of Little Bookham Street opposite Maddox Farm. In 1871 George Wales was a wood cutter here and by 1882 he had established himself as a wood dealer and carter. We shall meet more members of the Wales family in the next few photographs.

Shaftesbury Cottages, Little Bookham Street, c. 1900. This row of four cottages has a plaque with the name Shaftesbury Cottages and the date 1899. It is not known why they were given this name, but two of the cottages have remained in the same family ever since they were built by Alfred Wales, seen here with his family. He and his wife Polly moved into the end one when the cottages were finished and it now belongs to their grand-daughter, Grace, and one of her daughters lives in the third one. Although the Wales family was a large one, it did not include all these children! No doubt the posing for this photograph would have attracted the attention of other local children who were then assembled at the front. Alfred Wales is seen on the left with pipe in mouth and thumbs in lapels; his wife Polly is standing by the pony; and their son Ernest (Grace's father) is probably the lad seated above the wheel.

Polly Wales, the wife of Alfred Wales and Grace's grandmother. When she and Alfred lived in the cottage they used to keep pigs and chickens and grow all their own fruit and vegetables.

Minnie Wales with Lionel. Minnie was Ernest's wife and Grace's mother. Minnie and Ernest had three sons and four daughters, seen in the photograph on the next page.

The Wales family, *c.* 1917. This is the family of Ernest and Minnie Wales. Standing at the back are Jim, Elsie and May. Seated in front are Sid, Minnie with baby Lionel on her lap, then Grace and Edith. Grace recalls that the cottages all had outside toilets and very large gardens at the back. The front 'parlour' was only used for special occasions such as weddings or funerals.

Old Barn, Maddox Farm, Little Bookham, *c.* 1940. This farm of about eighty acres was on the west side of Little Bookham Street, just north of Maddox Lane: some of the buildings date from about 1650. At one time known as Petty's Farm, it has been known as Maddox Farm since 1870. It became a private residence in 1907.

Dawes Cottage, Little Bookham, 1909. Although this picture is entitled 'Old Cottages' and shows two front doors, it had been known as Dawes Cottage, with one household, since at least 1871. Major renovation in 1974 revealed evidence of an early fireplace with a bread oven.

Half Moon Cottage, Little Bookham Street, 1868. This cottage was once known as 'Rolts' and was built with timber felled in about 1500. In the 1871 census there were three households shown as occupants, so the people in this photograph may well be Jane Amey, a laundress; Mary Bowra, a retired domestic servant; and Susannah Wood with two of her children.

The Sole Farm Barn Mystery – 1906-1998. In 1906 the barn on the right was winched along rails from the roadside in front of the Old Barn Hall to a site just alongside. It was restructured and the house on this site was always referred to as 'the barn that was moved'. It was named Pitscottie and then The Moorings and later became Braithwaite's Engineering. However, when it was dismantled in 1998 no barn timbers were found! Where did they go? Below can be seen a photograph of Pitscottie.

PITSCOTTIE, GREAT BOOKHAM,
THE HOUSE THAT WAS MOVED

Sole Farm House, Great Bookham.

Sole Farm House, Great Bookham, *c.* 1910. This view is from the south east. Sole Farm is mentioned as early as 1337 and grew to be one of the largest farms in the parish – 390 acres in 1797. Arthur Bird purchased it in 1896 and sold the farm house as a private residence in 1905. The house and its old barn are all that remain of a once very significant farm.

Church Cottages, Great Bookham, 1920s. The external appearance of these cottages in Church Road has changed very little, though they are now hidden by trees and shrubs. The four cottages on the right, just north of the churchyard, were built in the seventeenth century on land which had been used previously as the slaughter yard for cattle belonging to the manor. Those on the left, lying back at a right-angle, were built in the early eighteenth century.

Hop Garden Cottage Great Bookham.

Hop Garden Cottage, Great Bookham, 1908. This cottage, now 191 Lower Road, is on the south side of the road. It was built in the late seventeenth or early eighteenth century and had hop gardens at the back. The building on the right is The Hermitage, which was smaller when Fanny Burney and her husband, General d'Arblay, lived there for a short time soon after their marriage in 1793. Their son was born there and baptized in St Nicolas' church.

Woodcote, Great Bookham, c. 1870. This house in Lower Road, made of brick and half-timbered, is part sixteenth- and part seventeenth-century. Originally it was a farm building on the Eastwick Park estate and the bull was kept in an adjacent building. At the time of this photograph a carrier, William Poulter, lived here and ran a cart twice a week to London.

Park Farm, Fetcham, 1924. The outbuildings of Park Farm seen here comprised the granary on staddle-stones to keep rats out, a barn, the slaughterhouse and stock buildings. The bailiff's house can be seen behind the trees on the right. All these buildings still exist in a private drive off The Ridgeway. The granary and other buildings still contain artefacts of past farming practices and the stock house has washing bowls and changing rooms that were used in former years by the polo teams whose grounds were there. The bailiff's house has been enlarged and is now called Quickset. The barn in the photograph below has been converted into an attractive country cottage called Quickset Barn and lovingly restored by the present owner.

Home Farm, Fetcham. This was one of the principal farms in Fetcham – a substantial building which was insured for £300 in 1800. Its main outbuildings, the dairy, hen house, stable, cow house, granary and barns, were grouped round the farmhouse off The Street. The barn in the background on the far left later became the Village Hall. The land was farmed by the Lang family from 1890: by William Lang, then by his son and finally by his grandson until 1936.

Home Farm workers. These workers are around one of William Lang's farm carts in Lodge Field, to the rear of the farmhouse. The man in the centre of the front row is Bill Brockhurst who was third gardener.

Garden Cottage, formerly Blacksmith's Cottage. Set back from The Street, just south of Cock Lane, is Garden Cottage which was a blacksmith's shop before 1690. It may well incorporate parts of a lime kiln, hence the peculiar chimney flue noticeable here. By 1791 a separate smithy existed closer to The Street which was used in 1859 by James Luff who was developing his business of 'Agricultural Machine Maker & General Smith, Gasfitter and Bell Hanger'.

Charlotte Luff. James Luff's business succeeded and in around 1866 the family moved into spacious new accommodation which they were to own, further north in The Street. After James retired, his son John ran the business until an unfortunate accident in which he was drowned. The business was taken over by Alfred Blaker in 1895 but the family remained there and John's daughter, Charlotte, lived there until the early 1930s.

Shamrock Cottage, Fetcham, *c.* 1900. Shamrock Cottage was the farm cottage for Pound Farm and existed until 1950 when it was replaced by shops. The only identifiable features in this photograph are the railway bridge and the triangle of land with the signpost at the junction of The Street and Cobham Road. This triangle was the northern tip of what was originally the pound for stray cattle which stretched back nearly to Cock Lane.

New Cottages, Fetcham, 1906. Opposite Shamrock Cottage are the New Cottages built around 1880 to replace ones set further back from the road. The message on the back of the postcard reads: 'This is a view of Auntie's house a young fellow took last Saturday. Those two children live over the road.'

Pound Farm, Fetcham, 1948. The name Pound Farm originated from what was originally the pound, mentioned opposite. The farmhouse, believed to be an 'improved' cottage, dated from the late seventeenth century, but all trace of it disappeared in 1950 after the building of Pound Crescent, Shamrock Close and the bungalows by the railway bridge.

Eve and Stan Harris, Fetcham, 1940s. The Harrises are on land belonging to Pound Farm, now Shamrock Close. This is the only photograph showing the pigsties of the former Pound Farm and the chalet-like structures in which people begged to be allowed to live during the housing shortage following the Second World War, before Leatherhead Urban District Council purchased the land to build the much-needed houses in 1950.

Monks Green Farm, Fetcham, c. 1920. On the map of 1777 on p. 2 this is shown as Monks Farm, at the extreme northern end of the village. There has been a farm here for at least 400 years. The present building was constructed around the chimney of a seventeenth-century farm in around 1740 and has later additions. It was farmed for the Lord of the Manor by tenants until 1895 when it was bought by William Smiles, a bank manager, and run as a dairy and stud farm until 1962. It is now a private residence.

Worple and Coombe Cottages, Fetcham, 1934. This photograph was taken while main drainage was being installed. Before the 1920s there were very few cottages in the Cobham Road, and Worple and Coombe Cottages are notable examples of timbering on the upper storey only. The 1791 survey shows them under the ownership of Cannon Farm, whose land extended from the river up to Cobham Road. (See map of 1777 on p. 2.)

Five
Trade and Transport

Fetcham post office, 1913. By the 1890s post office business was being handled by Angelina Partridge, wife of Henry Partridge who was the estate carpenter of Fetcham Park. They occupied this house with the quaint windows on the corner of The Ridgeway and Lower Road. Thus Fetcham's first (sub) post office building was established.

Fetcham post office, 1928. A close-up view of the old post office with a signpost pointing up The Ridgeway. The house originally seems to have been the lodge of Fetcham Park estate until a new one was built in the 1870s. Last occupied by Samuel Friston, it survived until 1928 when this photograph was taken.

St Clement's confectioner and tobacconist, Fetcham, c. 1930. On a map of 1914 a forge can be identified as being on the site of this shop in The Street. No picture of the forge has yet been found, but it was described as a 'dark, gloomy barn'. This picture is notable as it shows of the first real shop in Fetcham, opened by Arthur Miller and his wife in 1923.

Orchard Parade, Fetcham, c. 1935. An early extension to the shopping facilities was the construction of Orchard Parade in the Cobham Road in the early 1930s. It is shown in the photograph above not long after this date, with Hammond running the post office on the corner. Worple and Coombe cottages are in the background on the left and just this side of them is a sight rarely seen nowadays: a man up a ladder against a lamp-post. In front of the shops the trees planted by the verge are still very young. In the photograph below, some fifteen or twenty years later, they have matured, but unfortunately they fell victim to the axe later on.

Cordingley's shop, Great Bookham, *c.* 1890. This shop was on the corner of the High Street and Lower Road and William Cordingley came here to work as a plumber for George Baker in the 1870s. By the 1890s William Cordingley was running the firm which by then was known as Cordingley & Sons. He is seen here in front of the shop with his three daughters – Matilda, Annie and Bessie – and the men on the right are his two sons – Henry, also a plumber, and William, a house painter. The view below shows the shop in relation to the High Street and The Crown opposite, which was not set back from the crossroads as the present building is.

Great Bookham High Street, *c.* 1921. There was still no great danger from traffic in the High Street in those days! The Regency building on the extreme right has been a baker's shop since about 1900. The family grocery next door, Walker Smith's Stores, remained in business until after the end of the Second World War.

Aberdeen House, Great Bookham, 1904. Sidney Madge stands in front of his butcher's shop in Church Road, opposite the churchyard. It had been a butcher's shop run by George Peters since 1888 and there was a slaughter yard behind the shop which replaced the old Shamyard when Church Cottages were built across the road. The slaughter yard remained there until about 1955; the delicate cast ironwork above the portico was removed in 1966.

The post office, Great Bookham, c. 1910. There were three shops on the east side of Church Road beyond the churchyard. The building with the steps was the post office which was run by Edwin Bates, who was also a grocer and vendor of patent medicines; the left side was occupied by Walter Wood, bootmaker, and the adjacent building was a newsagent's and toy shop.

Simpson's Forge, Great Bookham, c. 1890. This forge was one of three or four in the village and was at Slinfold Cottage in Lower Road, near the crossroads. Mr Simpson also sold, hired and repaired bicycles, and stabled horses. There are iron wagon tyres by the door on the right and a tyring platform on the ground to the right of them. A similar tyring platform from Hamshar's forge, further along the road, is on display at the Leatherhead Museum.

Halfway House, Great Bookham, 1870. Edward Hamshar, the blacksmith referred to in the previous photograph, lived in this house in Lower Road, so this could well be him in the doorway with the three children. He also sold beer, assisted by his wife, Jane. When Edward died in 1893 his son, Thomas, took over the blacksmith trade.

McFarlane's dairy and milk cart, 1904. Halfway House was used for many trades. At this time the right-hand side of the house was used as a dairy by David McFarlane, seen here with his horse and milk cart. He moved later to Phoenice Farm in Dorking Road where he ran the dairy farm until it was taken over by Mr Marden in about 1929.

Halfway House, 1906. Before 1902 a builder called Stedman had run his business from this side of the house – his sign can be clearly seen in the photograph of this building in chapter 6. The new sign on the right 'BOOKHAM ....' appears to be the sign for the dairy in the photograph above. The young woman in the doorway is probably Mrs McFarlane who was twenty-four years old at that time.

Weale's shops, Little Bookham, c. 1915. Mary Weale's husband had been the landlord of the Windsor Castle pub, and she remained the licensee for some years after his death. In 1902 she set up a grocery and post office in the left-hand shop of the two shown here in Little Bookham Street; her coal merchant's business operated from the railway station yard. Her son, Frank, took over the coal merchant's business in about 1910 in the shop on the right.

The Elwyn Stores, Little Bookham, c. 1930. Mr A.J. Waits ran this grocery, off-licence and post office, well set back from the Guildford Road about 100 yards east of Woodlands Road. It was still a grocery, off-licence and post office in the 1960s. Since then it has been various restaurants and is currently an Indian restaurant called the Saffron Gardens.

Finch's Yard, Great Bookham, *c.* 1920. When Eastwick Park was sold in 1922, Walter Finch bought The Old Homestead in Eastwick Road and set up as a carrier. Haulage was all by horse and cart at that time and two of his young carters are here in the yard. Four generations of the same family have now been running the business. They still operate from the same site, but now specialize in transport of heavy machinery – no longer by horse!

Mr Longman and his cart, Great Bookham, 1935. F. Longman & Sons of Woodlands Road were smallholders and cartage contractors from around 1930. Mr Longman is seen here with his granddaughter, Celia, and his cart pulled by Daisy, at the junction by the church long before the need for a 'squareabout' and 'traffic calming'. The old elm and the walnut trees were still in the churchyard then.

Dr and Mrs Procter, Great Bookham, *c.* 1900. Dr Procter was the first car owner in Bookham. He came to live in the area in about 1894 and lived here for twenty-two years until his death in 1915 aged 52 years. He and his wife are seen here in their magnificent De Dion Bouton in front of The Croft in Church Road; the door on the right gave access to his surgery.

Bookham station, *c.* 1900. This view is looking westwards towards the station from the bend by today's National Trust car park in Church Road. The building on the left was the Merrylands Hotel, where the 'Photo-Me' works are now situated. The wrought-iron footbridge, which is still in use, can be seen on the right.

Bookham station under construction, early 1885. The station was opened by the London &
South Western Railway on 2 February 1885. Part of the new Guildford line connected with the
main Portsmouth line beyond Esher, with a spur from Effingham Junction through Bookham to
Leatherhead. This picture shows construction well advanced, and looks eastwards towards the
tunnel which was a condition of the Act authorizing the line.

Bookham station, 1885. This is looking westwards on opening day, 2 February 1885, or soon
afterwards. The train, with station staff and company officials, including two on the
locomotive, is at the 'up' platform and everything has been carefully posed for the occasion.
Initially there were only five weekday services from Guildford to Waterloo via Bookham, and
the journey took around $1\frac{1}{2}$ hours.

Bookham station, *c.* 1890. This is looking eastwards towards the tunnel. The signal box controlled the entrance to the goods yard to the right, not visible here. The yard closed in 1965 and the shed now contains offices and a builder's yard. This side of the station is the stationmaster's house – is he the man on the right with both hands on hips?

Bookham station, *c.* 1910. This is also looking eastwards towards the tunnel. The shrubs over the fence on this side of the stationmaster's house are noticeably more mature than in the photograph above taken at the end of the nineteenth century and there is now a neat flower bed on the platform side. Electrification of the line came in 1925 following the creation of the Southern Railway in 1923.

The bus depot, Fetcham, 1930. The Mizen brothers, who ran the watercress beds in Fetcham, sold land to the London General Omnibus Company for £3,800 in 1924 for the construction of a bus garage for their agents, the East Surrey Traction Company. This was to replace the inadequate facilities in the Swan Yard, Bull Yard and the Mid Surrey Motor Works. Part of the garage was in use by January 1925 and the complete depot was officially opened in June of that year. Built to take twenty-four vehicles, it was already too small by 1927 when a third section was added and the existing roof raised to take double-decker buses. This photograph shows the recently extended building with a fine array of buses on display. The depot is now another piece of history as the entire garage was demolished in May 1999 and the site is being developed for new offices.

Six

Inns, Hotels and Tea Houses

The Cock Inn, Fetcham, 1759. This is a painting by Dominic Serres. The inn was on the corner of Cock Lane and The Street and is shown on the 1777 map of Fetcham on p. 2. This view shows the rear view of the inn – its licence was not renewed from 1810 onwards, so this painting is the only existing view of it. Queen Elizabeth I is said to have drunk mead there when she visited Slyfield Manor, but there is no firm evidence for this! After ceasing to be an inn it was divided into two cottages – Yew Tree and Tea Tree cottages.

The Green Domino, Fetcham. Just west of the Leatherhead bridge stood Fetcham Grove House, described in the 1780s as 'a square brick house'. Various extensions were added to it, but it was unoccupied in 1915 so it was used for billeting soldiers. Later on it became the Green Domino café, though it is not known why it was given this name. After the café closed it was occupied by Bishop's removal firm until it was demolished in 1998.

The old Rising Sun, a Grade II listed building at the junction of Cobham Road with Guildford Road, *c.* 1905. It remained a public house until the new Rising Sun (now a 'Harvester') opened across the road in the 1930s. It then became successively a café, youth hostel and then a restaurant which it has remained ever since, albeit of different ethnic cuisines.

The Rising Sun, Fetcham, *c.* 1900. The Rising Sun was described in 1805 as 'A compact brewhouse, storeroom and cellar capable of holding 78 butts of beer', i.e. 8,424 gallons! For many years there was a sign on the outside wall saying '*c.* 1348'. The medieval core of the building is considered to be about 8.64m by 5.6m with a crown post roof, apparently supported by timber framework and stone walling, probably much extended in about 1800. One possible origin of the building is that it was a priest's house for the still unplaced 'Chappelle of St Kateryn's' of 1528, though this may refer to St Catherine's Chapel in Fetcham parish church. Cyclists, three of whom are seen here, gained the reputation in the early 1900s of being the 'road hogs' of the day as far as local communities were concerned.

Four sketches of the Rising Sun interior, done by Mr Langdon in 1955 from pictures of earlier days when the Rising Sun was a café/restaurant.

Somehow one cannot help feeling that these views depict scenes more in keeping with the age and style of the building than the present Chinese restaurant, elegant though the latter is.

Mr Tompkins' Tea Shop & Shamrock Tea Gardens, Fetcham, *c.* 1935. Notice the poster advertising a film at the Crescent Cinema in Leatherhead. Mr Tompkins lived in Shamrock Cottage (seen in Chapter 4) during the 1930s and '40s and had his tea shop, advertising choc ices, in the building next door. This picture was taken in the heyday of cycle touring and, as can be seen below, there was a large garden at the back which provided tables and chairs for the weekend visitors from London and other areas. This became the principal meeting place for cyclists after Rivermead House in River Lane was destroyed by a fire in 1936. How delightful it looks!

The Bell Inn, Fetcham, *c.* 1930. The presence of a hostelry or inn on the corner of Bell Lane can be traced back to before the eighteenth century, as can be judged by the foundations, and by the finds of bottles and sherds in a nearby pond. The building in this photograph dates from the early nineteenth century – it provided a meeting place for the Hunt and a venue for wedding receptions and other events. It was replaced by the present building in 1932.

The Anchor, Great Bookham, *c.* 1905. This inn in the Lower Road was built in the seventeenth century and was known as the Red Lion until the end of the eighteenth century. Census returns from 1841 record a beer retailer in Eastwick, and an inn called The Anchor was licensed in 1881. The Anchor was part of the Eastwick estate sold by William Keswick in 1918 when it was recorded as being 'let to the Swan Brewery Company (Leatherhead) Ltd.'

The Victoria Hotel, and former Saracen & Ring, Great Bookham, 1905. The Victoria Hotel is seen straight ahead on the corner of the High Street and the Guildford Road. As can be seen, the Guildford Road did not cut this area off as it does now, but did an S bend at this point. On the left, the fence marks the boundary of Bookham Grove, and on the right, Grove Cottages were formerly an inn known originally as The White Hart. When Viscount Downe acquired the Bookham Grove estate in 1775 the inn became the Saracen and Ring to commemorate an ancestor of his who had fought in the Crusades. He slew a Saracen and also a lion and presented its paw to the king. In return the king gave him a ring and granted him the right to have a crest bearing a Saracen with a ring and a lion's paw. However, in 1895, that ardent temperance worker, Mrs Chrystie, bought the premises and resold them as private dwellings.

The Victoria Hotel and Cyclists' Rest, Great Bookham, *c.* 1920. This was built by Mrs Chrystie as a temperance hotel in 1896; it advertised luncheons, teas and dinners as well as accommodation. From the turn of the century up to the outbreak of the Second World War people flocked in droves to Bookham either by train or bicycle for walks or cycling tours to visit Bookham Common, Ranmore and other beauty spots. It remained a hotel until the 1950s.

The Royal Oak, Great Bookham, *c.* 1890. This appears to be the only photograph of the Royal Oak in existence, and only the sign is really visible. Parts of the building date from the fifteenth century and it was a beer house, probably owned by a farm belonging to Eastwick Park to brew and provide beer for the workers. In 1628 the Royal Oak paid a rental to the Manor of Eastwick on the feast day of St John the Baptist of 'a red rose and a quart of Lamphreys'.

The Crown Inn, Great Bookham, *c.* 1900. The Crown was right in the centre of the village at the crossroads, opposite the parish church. It was recorded in a survey in 1777 and there are several further references to it in directories and census returns throughout the nineteenth century. Arthur Clapshaw, the proprietor during the first decade of the twentieth century, changed its image from an inn to a 'Family and Commercial Hotel'.

The Crown Inn, *c.* 1909. Frank Wigley took over as proprietor and the hotel continued to provide luncheons, dinners, teas, good beds and beer from the Hodgson Kingston Brewery. Sadly, this picturesque vernacular old building with its attractive barge-boarding was demolished in 1932 and (ironically) replaced by the 'Old Crown' public house.

Halfway House, Great Bookham, *c*. 1895. This building has already appeared in chapters 4 and 5, but here we see it as an alehouse, with its brewing chimney. The sign over the door is advertising 'Fine Ales and London Porter'. It was probably Edward Hamshar, blacksmith and beer retailer, standing in the doorway in 1870, and in this photograph it may well be his widow, Jane, who remained as the beer retailer after his death in 1893 until her death in 1902. Mrs Chrystie then bought the house and closed this ale house also.

Merrylands Hotel, Great Bookham, *c*. 1905. Mrs. Chrystie built this hotel opposite the station towards the turn of the 19th century to provide (temperance!) accommodation and tea rooms for the many visitors from London at that time. To give some idea of this, the hotel could seat 200 people in the dining room and there were tea houses for 1,000 children and 300 adults. The site became a factory during the First World War and engineering works were built in the garden.

The Windsor Castle, Little Bookham, 1868. Henry Weale became the publican around this time and ran the inn for about twenty years. After his death his widow, Mary Ann Weale, remained the licensee until 1902. Weale's shop which she then opened further down Little Bookham Street developed from the shop which she ran here which can be seen on the right-hand side of the inn.

The Windsor Castle, 1913. Although this is a sixteenth-century building, its first recorded use as a public house was not until 1806. At different times it has been called the Castle, the Windsor Castle and Ye Olde Windsor Castle and has recently reverted to the latter.

Fireplace of the Windsor Castle, 1926. This is an old fireplace in what was called Ye Olde Windsor Castle at that time. This fireplace was on the right hand wall of the front room, entered then through the front door which was on the left of the inn. Most of the surround of this fireplace is still visible.

The Wayside Tea House, Little Bookham, 1934. This bungalow, still called Wayside, is on the Guildford Road next door to what was then the Elwyn Stores, now Saffron Gardens. Tea houses such as these were enormously popular in the 1930s, both with the many cyclists and also new owners of cars who would 'go for a spin' and stop somewhere like this for tea. The Wayside tea rooms were run by John and Lilian Earley in 1934, but had closed by 1937.

THE CLIFF TEA HOUSE,
GUILDFORD ROAD,
BOOKHAM,
Nr Leatherhead, SURREY.
Propr W. J. Wheeker.

Luncheons and Teas, Minerals & Cigarettes.
⚜ Parties Catered for ⚜
Excellent Parking Accommodation for Cars,
Attractive Grounds.

The Cliff Tea House, Little Bookham, *c.* 1935. The house was built in 1922 just west of Chalkpit Lane with access from Guildford Road, where 'Twin Gates' is now. William Wheeker owned the house, Whitecliff, in the early 1930s and his tea rooms continued under the next owner, Cyril Short, until the end of the decade.

Seven
Churches

St Nicolas' church, Great Bookham, Sunday 29 April 1923. The Duke and Duchess of York (future King George VI and Queen Elizabeth) are leaving the church after attending morning service while on their honeymoon at Polesden Lacey. They are accompanied by the rector's Warden, Stanley Russell of Elmcroft, and the people's Warden, Sidney Madge, the butcher.

Sketch of the East End of Great Bookham Church Surrey

St Nicolas' church, Great Bookham, 1846. A sketch of the east end of the church made by William Leach, who lived across the road at The Hermitage. It shows the north aisle just after it had been rebuilt and enlarged between 1841 and 1845 to provide extra seats required by the vicar, William Heberden, 'to disarm pretexts for dissent'! The chancel window, also new in 1841, is alleged to be a copy of the fourteenth-century design.

St Nicolas' church, 1866. This view from the south east shows the fine Perpendicular window in the east end of the south aisle (the Slyfield Chapel). At one time this window was filled in and there is a painting of the church in 1829 with the window blocked up. The present window was installed in 1859 and the glass was given in memory of Lord Raglan, of Crimean War fame.

St Nicolas' church, 1905. This view from the south west shows the ivy-covered stone base of the tower which was built in the late twelfth century: the buttresses were added in the fifteenth century. The remaining part of the Norman south aisle (c. 1140) can be seen next to the tower – it was only 5ft 9in wide. The timber bell-tower, surmounted by an elegant spire, originally had four bells, one of which was cast in 1675, but now it only has two.

St Nicolas' church, *c.* 1890. This photograph was taken before the lych-gate was built in 1897. On the right is the sign for the Crown Inn with the landlord's name, W. Clapshaw, on it. The pollarded tree at the corner of the churchyard was an elm recorded as having been planted by Churchwarden Ralph Hilder in 1627; it succumbed to Dutch elm disease in 1977. The tree on the right was one of five planted by the Revd Samuel L'Isle in 1733.

St Nicolas' church, 1909. Several changes have occurred since the photograph above was taken. The lych-gate was erected in 1897 by public subscription to celebrate the Diamond Jubilee of Queen Victoria. Not only has the lych-gate appeared, but also a telegraph pole. The gas lamp (with ladder against it) has been moved from inside the churchyard to the pavement by the signpost which is also new. The boy and girl were probably posed for the photograph.

St Nicolas' church interior, *c.* 1910. The arcades on either side of the nave are different in style: the south is late Norman (*c.* 1140) whilst the north is Transitional (*c.* 1180). The glass in the chancel window was destroyed during the Second World War by blast from a bomb; six panels of fifteenth-century Flemish glass were purchased as a replacement in 1954.

St Nicolas' church interior, *c.* 1920. The south aisle, widened in the fifteenth century, can be glimpsed through the south arcade. The bowl of the font is Norman (*c.* 1190) and was moved from the north aisle in 1885 to stand in the nave on a new base and stem.

Little Bookham parish church, 1902. The church did not receive its dedication to All Saints until long after this date. Since the end of the fifteenth century the church has consisted of a nave and chancel under one continuous roof, with a porch added in 1901, just one year before this photograph. To the right of the porch door, the in-filled arcades of a former south aisle can be seen in the wall. The east window of the chancel is based on a thirteenth-century design. The large chest tomb, to the right, was for Major General Coote Manningham, who died in 1809: his wife was the fourth daughter of the Revd George Pollen who was rector and Lord of the Manor of Little Bookham until his death in 1812.

Little Bookham parish church, *c.* 1921. The magnificent yew tree, with the seat running all round it, is considered to be about 700 years old. It is obscuring the view of the wooden bell-turret with its single bell, but the vestries on the left and the porch on the right can clearly be seen.

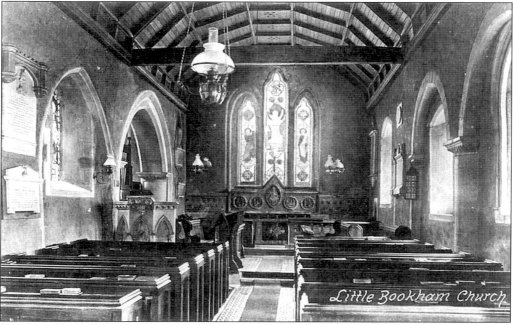

Little Bookham church interior, 1906. The round pillars and square capitals which supported the arches of the early arcade can be seen best in the south wall on the right. The arch in the north wall of the chancel (behind the pulpit) leads to the organ chamber which was added in 1901. The pulpit is decorated with seventeenth-century carved panels.

The Memorial Hall, Great Bookham, 1912. This building was erected in Lower Road in memory of Mary Chrystie who did so much for the local community. It was known as the Memorial Hall and later became the Baptist church.

Stone-laying ceremony at the Baptist church, Great Bookham, 1929. Here we see people listening to the opening address at the stone-laying ceremony described opposite.

The stone-laying ceremony at Great Bookham Baptist church. In 1925 the Memorial Hall was hired by George Cook JP of Sole Farm House for Sunday evening services, and later purchased and converted into a Baptist church. The first service in the new church was held in January 1928 with Mr Cook as the pastor. New premises for youth work and a Sunday school were soon needed and a site on the west side of the church was acquired. A large crowd of men, women and children are seen here at the stone-laying ceremony on the site, with the scaffold poles bedecked with flags for the occasion.

The Congregational Mission Hall, Great Bookham, c. 1900. 'Congregationalists' began to meet in people's homes around 1890. A preaching station was established in Church Road in 1895 and a Mission Hall was erected. John Ansell, seen here in front of the hall, was appointed Missioner: he lived in a house in Sole Farm Road which was built behind the hall in about 1899.

The opening of the Congregational church, Great Bookham, 1929. In 1922 discussions began on the need for a new and larger site for a new church building to replace the Mission Hall, and in 1928 a site was acquired in Eastwick Road. Church members are seen here at the opening ceremony on 17 July 1929. The church had seating for 120 people as well as a vestry, church parlour, kitchen and toilets.

St Mary's church, Fetcham, 1809. This is from an aquatint and is one of the few early paintings known of the church still known to exist. It is not known who painted it – J.M.W. Turner is believed to have sketched several scenes in Fetcham when he visited the area, but this is not reputed to be by him. At this time the fabric of the church was in very poor condition. The Norman south aisle had collapsed during the early eighteenth century and in 1760 the wall was blocked in under the arches. Over 100 years later the aisle was rebuilt as one of the many improvements effected by the Revd Sir Edward Graham Moon during his forty-five years as rector from 1859 to 1904. Other improvements carried out during his time included extensive repairs to the roof and walls and the installation of larger windows to provide more light. Most of the stained glass windows are memorials to the Moon family, including the great east window, dedicated to the rector.

St Mary's church, *c.* 1870. This view from the south-west corner shows the church before the south aisle was rebuilt and the tower covered with ivy.

St Mary's church. This photograph must have been taken prior to 1905, when the lych-gate was built as one of the memorials to the Revd Sir Edward Graham Moon. The boundary hedge to the churchyard was replaced by a brick wall which also enclosed an extension to the churchyard to the southern boundary with the Dell.

St Mary's church, *c.* 1925. This is the ivy-covered north aspect of the church, showing the access from Fetcham Park House at the end of the private drive. The steps and gas lamp are still there, but the steps were sealed off by gates in 1930 when the church drive was completed from the Lower Road and The Ridgeway.

St Mary's church, 1957. This photograph was taken before the Church Hall was built on the land in the foreground. There was much opposition to this at first in neighbouring roads, but permission to build the hall was eventually granted in 1969 and four years later it was dedicated. Proceeds from the sale of Charity Land behind the village school assisted with the cost and the land is now part of the school's recreation area.

The lych-gate, 1906. This gate was erected as a memorial to the Revd E.G. Moon and given by his widow. The message on the back of this postcard dated the same year says: 'I know you will like this. N.B. This was erected for Sir E. Moon.' Access to the lych-gate was through the stable yard of Fetcham Park House and up an old track to the west of the church.

Interior of St Mary's church. During the incumbency of Canon Douglas Bryant (1974-1987) the stone pulpit seen here was removed and a new oak one erected close to the chancel arch. The war memorial plaque was relocated in the south transept and the fine chancel screen in this picture was removed. The church was redecorated and the murals in blue and silver above the east window were obliterated, much to the regret of many.

The chancel at St Mary's, before electric lighting was installed in 1926. The Victorian decoration of the windows and rebates can clearly be seen here. These are the murals referred to above which were later painted over. The presence of floral decoration suggests a festival, but the accent on tropical plants is puzzling.

A disastrous fire on Shrove Tuesday 1987 completely gutted the Roman Catholic church of the Holy Spirit in Fetcham, barely twenty years after its dedication in 1968. Amazingly, the church was rebuilt in time to celebrate Midnight Mass on Christmas Eve the same year. The photograph below shows the interior; the blackened Madonna, statue of St Joseph and Stations of the Cross have been retained as reminders of the fire.

Eight
Education

Great Bookham Elementary School, 1915. The school was built in 1856 by the Dawney family in memory of the 7th Viscount Downe of Bookham Grove. It was originally known as St James' School: it then became a 'National' School, i.e. a Church of England school under the National Society for the Education of the Poor. The school building is in the centre and on the right is the master's house. The extension on the left was added in 1910.

Great Bookham National School, 1895. In the school log book during the 1890s the master, William Vellender, complained frequently about the boys' absenteeism for truancy and agricultural work. However, two years after this photograph was taken he wrote 'Some days there were over seventy boys present and I found that with no help I had quite enough to do to keep them all at work.' I should think he did!

Great Bookham National School, c. 1900. William Vellender, on the left, was still master. It was a time when the number of pupils was increasing, but the building was deteriorating. An inspection report in 1904 commented 'The midden closets are very poor indeed and smelt very badly ... the ventilation in the common classroom is very bad.' However, although the building left a lot to be desired, the school itself was doing well.

Great Bookham Elementary School, 1919. After the Education Act of 1902 the National Schools were taken over by Surrey County Council. This school then became an Elementary School and this is a class of pupils with their teacher, Mrs Slimmins. From left to right, front row: Ethel Simms, Doris Reid, Evelyn Russell, Louise and Phyllis Rollins, Edith and Alice Butcher, Marie Absolam. Second row: Bobby Worrall, ? Harris, Reg Elms, Raymond Longhurst, ? Wales, Billy Knight and brother, Dick Handley, Lily Geeson. Third row: Leonard Rollinson, Margery Robinson, Dora Butler, Mary Smith, ? Parker, Clare Tanner, Violet Broid, Violet and Kathleen Wales, Eva Cottee, Sybil Faux, Fred Hart. Fourth row: Ronald Wright, Harry Ranger, ? Tilley, Fred Marks, John Miller, W. Widdy, Jim Edwards. Back row: June Handley, Gladys Stevens, -?-, Emily Ayres, Betty Bye, Winnie Stemp, Phyllis Wales.

Great Bookham National School, *c.* 1900. It is interesting to see that there were as many girls in a class as there were boys. Regular visits to the school were made by Mrs Mary Chrystie, who was one of the School Managers and came regularly to inspect the girls' needlework and to listen to their singing, reading and recitations. At about this time she presented Blanche Batchelor with a book as a reward for intelligent answers during her visit. Is Blanche in this photograph?

Eastwick School, Great Bookham, 1895. This is a class of what were known as 'Mixed Infants'. The school was built in Eastwick Road in 1830 and enlarged in 1882. The average daily attendance was recorded as fifty-eight and census returns show that there were two teachers there as early as 1871. The school was found to be in poor condition at its inspection in 1907 and was sold by its trustees in about 1912.

Woodfield Private School, Bookham.

Woodfield School, Little Bookham, 1909. On the left is the house in which a Miss Smith ran a small private school for children up to the age of ten years: the house stands on the south side of the junction of Sole Farm Road with Little Bookham Street. Presumably the children in the photograph were the pupils at the school.

Manor House School, Little Bookham, *c.* 1940. Miss Green and Miss Wheeler established a girls' boarding school in Sidmouth in 1921 which moved to Mickleham Hall in 1930. They then bought Little Bookham Manor House in 1937 which was for sale after Henry Court Willcock Pollen's death in 1934. They added a new block on the west side for a gym, with dormitories above so that the school could accommodate about sixty boarders. It is now mainly a day school.

The School of Stitchery and Lace, Great Bookham, c. 1940. A school of stitchery and lace was founded in Leicester in 1927 by Miss Julia Sweet with just a few girls. Within ten years she had acquired The Grange in Rectory Lane and by 1960 about 50 girls could be accommodated. In 1964 the school changed its name to the School of Stitchery, with the addition of sheltered workshops. In the photograph below the girls and a teacher can be seen working in one of the elegant rooms inside The Grange. On the right beside the wall is a beautiful lace canopy over a baby's crib.

The Spinney, Great Bookham, c. 1935. The Spinney School was a private school in Eastwick Drive for boys from three to eight years and on to twelve years for girls. This was started by the Misses Dorothy and Eleanor Joce in 1931. The property had originally belonged to Eastwick Park (by this time Southey Court School) and many of the boys went on to Southey Court and the girls to Manor House School. In 1950 Miss Joan Linday took over the school until its closure in 1967.

The Spinney from the garden. The house and two barns had originally been cowsheds which were converted into a house with a rose garden, tennis lawn, kitchen garden and orchard. The house was demolished in the 1960s.

Southey Hall School, Great Bookham, *c.* 1935. This building is the former Eastwick Park which became a preparatory school for boys run by Mr Henry Fussell who moved his school here from Worthing in 1930. During the Second World War the school was evacuated down to Devon in 1940 and the Canadian Army occupied the building. The school returned after the war, but it closed a few years later and the house was demolished in the 1950s. A former pupil has provided some of the information about the following photographs of the interior of the school.

Southey Hall School recreation room, *c.* 1935. This was formerly the ballroom of Eastwick Park, and the former pupil wrote: 'At the end of the Christmas term everyone had a part in the pantomime. A stage was erected in the ballroom.... The audience had two thirds, the stage in the other third. Behind the stage was the door to the dining room [seen below] where we changed and prepared for our entry on stage.'

The dining room. All sixty boys and six staff ate in this room. 'Supper at 6.30 consisted of bread, butter and jam and quantities of tea. This meal was always better at the beginning of term and at half-term when we had the cakes we brought back with us, sent by our mothers.'

Fetcham Village School, c. 1904. The original building was erected in 1854 on land given by the Hankey family of Fetcham Park. This was to be a Church of England school run by the parish church, not under the 'National Society'. Alongside the school was the master's house, rent-free and furnished. When the school opened there were sixty-one pupils on the register. Later additions were made in 1872 and 1886 to include an infants' class and to provide separate entrances for the boys and the girls. Classes were always held separately for boys and girls in all church schools and were regarded as separate schools, although housed in the same building, and the infants were also a separate school. The bell tower seen in this photograph has since been removed.

Fetcham Boys' School, 1892. Included among the names of boys in this photograph are three that are on the 1914-1918 War Memorial in Fetcham parish church – John and Albert Diment and Alfred Alexander. Mr Constable, the master, was a pillar of the community and, amongst other duties, was the post office representative. From left to right, front row: ? West, Percy Maspero, A. Ginger, Max Sanders, Jack Diment, Bert Stovell, David Simmons, Bert Pinion, ? Summerfield, Bert Diment. Middle row: Harry Harding, Ernest Maspero, George Bullham, Edgar and Reuben Sanders, Harry Botting, Sid Alexander, Albert Walters, Tom Hillyer, Bert Drewitt, Fred Cooper, Bill Hendry, Bill Summers, Wallis Maspero. Back row: Joe Hamblin, George Hart, George Penfold, Bill Belton, Jesse Lemon, Mr Constable, Ralph King, Bob Cooper, Philip Sargent, Jim Hillyer.

Fetcham Village School, 1910. The board being held by the girl in the centre is labelled 'Fetcham C.E. School, Group II, 1910.' Neither the names of the pupils or the teachers have been provided, but the boy in the centre of the middle row is Harold Sainsbury, now ninety years of age.

Fetcham Village School, 1926. By this time the school was known as St Mary's. Another photograph without names. Can any reader identify any of the pupils?

Badingham College, Fetcham, 1954. (Photographs of the building are also shown on p. 41 under Fetcham Park.) It was in 1924 after the death of John Barnard Hankey that Fetcham Park was bought by the Revd J. Wilkie to become a boys' boarding school. He named it Badingham College after the Suffolk village where he had been rector. The school closed in about 1964 when the house and grounds were sold for development.

The entrance hall, Badingham College, 1954. This must have been a most imposing entrance hall, both as a school and as a private residence.

Ceiling painting at Badingham College, 1954. This early eighteenth-century painting by Louis Laguerre (1633-1721) is on the ceiling of the Shell Room, which has been expertly cleaned and restored to become a feature of the mansion.

Nine

Recreation and Special Events

Ladies' stoolball team, Little Bookham, 1912. The *Lady's Pictorial* published an illustrated article on 27 July 1912: 'A "Grand Match at Stoolball" was played at Little Bookham near Leatherhead recently between Mrs Willcock Pollen's Stool-ball Club and a team of the Effingham Cricket Club.' From left to right, back row: Umpire, Miss Coleman, -?-, Miss Longhurst, Mrs Russell, Mrs West, Mrs Choules. Front row: Mrs Chipping, Mrs Longhurst, Mrs Willcock Pollen, Mrs Wales, -?-, Mrs Paris.

Stoolball, Little Bookham, 1912. Miss Coleman is on the left and Miss Longhurst on the right. After an exciting contest, the ladies won the match by nine runs, scoring 94 to their opponents' 85. The highest scorers were Miss Longhurst with 22 runs and Miss Coleman with 20.

Men's stoolball team, Little Bookham, 1912. The men were captained by Mr Willcock Pollen and had to play left-handed. Although the names of nearly all the ladies have been recorded, apart from the captain, those of the men are not known, and there is nothing to say which of them was Mr Willcock Pollen. He was Lord of the Manor and was living at The Old Rectory at this time, where the match was played.

Stoolball, Little Bookham, 1930. Mrs Willcock Pollen, in the centre of the back row, is still involved, but may no longer be a player at the age of sixty-three years. There are no fewer than six members of the Longhurst family here, including little Dennis at the front. Mrs Edith Russell (*née* Longhurst) is at the right-hand end of the back row – is she the Miss E. Longhurst who batted so well in 1912?

Country dancing at Little Bookham, 1920s. Miss Bliss, who lived at Bayfield, organised this country dance session on the lawn in front of the tithe barn of Manor Farm opposite Little Bookham Manor House. From the left, the ladies are Mrs Harrison, Miss Collins, -?-, Mrs Jolley, Mrs Russell and Mrs Worsell.

A charabanc outing from the Windsor Castle, *c.* 1911. These annual 'chara' outings were very popular with customers who saved up for them all year. For many, it was their only visit to the sea or other places of interest. The landlord, William Wickens, is in front of the charabanc with twenty-five of his customers. Where were they going? A trip to Brighton or Worthing would be an endurance test on those solid tyres! Was the lone female Mrs Wickens? She ran the Windsor Castle after her husband died.

Great Bookham Silver Band, *c.* 1905. This band, the forerunner of the present Mole Valley Silver Band, rehearsed and gave concerts in the Victoria Hall in East Street from the early 1900s until the First World War. In the summer it played for dances on the lawns of houses such as Eastwick Park, Bookham Grove, Ballingvey and Bookham Gables. Dances were also held at the recreation ground.

The Old Barn Hall, Great Bookham, 1906. Arthur Bird's project to convert a barn in Church Road into a village hall was implemented by Richard Lee, a Great Bookham architect; Messrs Cummins & Son, a Dorking builder's firm, did the conversion. The main framework of the barn with its tiled roof was retained. Brickwork was laid between the old oak piers and dormer windows were inserted in the roof.

The Old Barn Hall interior, 1906. The hall was furnished to seat 300 people and had three large exits. A moveable stage was erected at the end opposite the porch entrance, and Mrs Bird gave a piano. Behind the stage were dressing rooms, lavatories, a kitchen and a store-house. The floral decorations may be those which were provided for the Opening Ceremony on Empire Day, 1906.

Visit of Duke and Duchess of York to Great Bookham, 1923. On 26 April George, Duke of York (the future King George VI) and Lady Elizabeth Bowes-Lyon were married and went to Polesden Lacey for part of their honeymoon. In the late afternoon, the Duke and Duchess were driven from the station along Church Road to St Nicolas' church where the chairman of the Parish Council, Mr D.W. McFarlane, presented a loyal address. Scouts, guides, and boys from Dr Barnardo's Home at Epsom lined the road outside the church.

The Surrey Union Hunt kennels, Great Bookham, 1905. These kennels were on the east side of the Dorking Road where the Kenilworth Equestrian Centre is now. In the nineteenth century Surrey had three hunts – the Surrey, the Surrey Union, and the Hambledon. The Surrey Union hunted over the centre of the county from Kingston to Reigate, and meets were held in both Bookham and Fetcham.

The Meet at the Bell Inn, Fetcham

A Hunt meet at the old Bell Inn, Fetcham, *c.* 1915. The Bell Inn was a popular place to hold a meet. The old building was situated sufficiently far back from Bell Lane to accommodate the Surrey Union Hunt which, by the early 1900s, was based in Bookham, with a complement of about forty-eight pairs of hounds. The cottage in the background was variously known as Chain Cottage, Huntsman's Cottage or Coachman's House.

A Hunt meet at Rising Sun, Fetcham, *c.* 1940. This was another popular venue for a meet. This photograph must have been taken soon after the beginning of the Second World War before the threat of invasion prompted the removal of signposts. The old Rising Sun can be seen in the background. Also noticeable, running across the photograph, is the railway embankment bereft of trees – probably a precaution against fire rather than leaves on the line!

A charabanc outing from the old Rising Sun, Fetcham, 1922. Just as the Windsor Castle ran their annual charabanc outings, so did the old Rising Sun in Fetcham. Unfortunately, there are no names for this group. Can any readers identify any of them?

The new Rising Sun darts team, Fetcham, c. 1950. The successful darts team outside the new Rising Sun, now a 'Harvester', display their trophy and also their 'ockey' – the marker placed on the floor from where the players throw the darts. Sadly, this is another group for which no names have been recorded.

Stage end of Fetcham Village Hall

A century ago a fine barn, now the beautiful

FETCHAM VILLAGE HALL

This very attractive Hall seating 280 is

Available for Letting

Large Stage with full modern Lighting

Cloak Rooms and Dressing Rooms

Lavishly Equipped Kitchen

Magnificent Maple Dancing Floor

For terms for Letting for
DANCES : THEATRICALS : MEETINGS
WHIST DRIVES : BAZAARS : GAMES
Write or 'phone : H. R. Franklin,
The Spinney, Lower Road, Fetcham

Fetcham Village Hall, 1935. The Fetcham Women's Institute was founded in 1927 and used to meet in the Reading Room. By about 1930 they needed a larger hall, so the century-old barn of Home Farm was purchased and converted into a village hall, mainly by volunteers, and was opened in May 1933. It has been in constant use by many groups ever since.

Mr Cayman, bee keeper, c. 1930. Mr Cayman lived in Cobham Road and was a dedicated bee keeper. He is seen here searching for the queen bee and appears to be covered in bees. He evidently disdained to wear even gloves, never mind any sort of protective face covering! In the photograph below, the other members of the bee-keeping fraternity, seen here having tea, do seem to have had some form of head and face protection.

Cyclists on Hawks Hill, 1917. Here are four cyclists, three of whom have dismounted, presumably for the photograph. The fourth one toiling up behind the others appears to have a heavy load in his front basket – possibly a picnic. As explained earlier, cyclists were regarded as the 'road hogs' of the early twentieth century, but compared to the 'ton up' boys of today, these four do not seem to pose too much of a threat!

A Victory street party, Fetcham, 1945. Street parties were held all over the country to celebrate the end of the war. It is not known whether this one was to celebrate VE Day for the end of the war in Europe, or VJ Day for the end of the war in Japan, but it was held in Cannonside and a good time was being had by all, in spite of stringent food rationing still in operation.

The Opening of Young Street, 1941. Young Street, which is near the boundary between Bookham and Fetcham, seems a good place to end this book. It was built by Canadian soldiers based here during the war to enable military vehicles to avoid bottlenecks of places like Redhill, Reigate and Leatherhead. The road was finished in the summer of 1941 and Mr King, the Prime Minister of Canada, is seen here opening it on 28 August 1941. Years later it was named Young Street after Major Young who was in charge of the soldiers who constructed the road.

The Leatherhead & District Local History Society is always glad to receive any photographs or written records of the area, either as a gift or a loan. If you have old photographs of interest, please contact the Records Secretary, c/o the Leatherhead Museum, Hampton Cottage, 64 Church Street, Leatherhead KT22 8DP. Tel: 01372 386348.